Daniel Corkery

THE IRISH WRITERS SERIES
James F. Carens, General Editor

TITLE	*AUTHOR*
SEAN O'CASEY	Bernard Benstock
J. C. MANGAN	James Kilroy
W. R. RODGERS	Darcy O'Brien
STANDISH O'GRADY	Phillip L. Marcus
PAUL VINCENT CARROLL	Paul A. Doyle
SEUMAS O'KELLY	George Brandon Saul
SHERIDAN LEFANU	Michael Begnal
AUSTIN CLARKE	John Jordan
BRIAN FRIEL	D. E. S. Maxwell
DANIEL CORKERY	George Brandon Saul
EIMAR O'DUFFY	Robert Hogan
MERVYN WALL	Robert Hogan
FRANK O'CONNOR	James Matthews
JOHN BUTLER YEATS	Douglas Archibald
LORD EDWARD DUNSANY	Zack Bowen
MARIA EDGEWORTH	James Newcomer
MARY LAVIN	Zack Bowen
OSCAR WILDE	Edward Partridge
SOMERVILLE AND ROSS	John Cronin
SUSAN L. MITCHELL	Richard M. Kain
J. M. SYNGE	Robin Skelton
KATHARINE TYNAN	Marilyn Gaddis Rose
LIAM O'FLAHERTY	James O'Brien
IRIS MURDOCH	Donna Gerstenberger
JAMES STEPHENS	Birgit Bramsbäck
BENEDICT KIELY	Daniel Casey
EDWARD MARTYN	Robert Christopher
DOUGLAS HYDE	Gareth Dunleavy
EDNA O'BRIEN	Grace Eckley
CHARLES LEVER	M. S. Elliott
BRIAN MOORE	Jeanne Flood
SAMUEL BECKETT	Clive Hart
ELIZABETH BOWEN	Edwin J. Kenney
JOHN MONTAGUE	Frank Kersnowski
ROBERT MATURIN	Robert E. Lougy
GEORGE FITZMAURICE	Arthur E. McGuinness
MICHAEL MCLAVERTY	Leo F. McNamara

FRANCIS STUART	J. H. Natterstad
PATRICK KAVANAGH	Darcy O'Brien
BRINSLEY MACNAMARA AND GEORGE SHIELS	Raymond J. Porter
STEPHEN MACKENNA	Roger Rosenblatt
JACK B. YEATS	Robin Skelton
WILLIAM ALLINGHAM	Alan Warner
SAMUEL LOVER	Mabel Worthington
FLANN O'BRIEN	Bernard Benstock
DENIS JOHNSTON	James F. Carens
WILLIAM LARMINIE	Richard J. Finneran
SIR SAMUEL FERGUSON	Malcolm Brown
LADY GREGORY	Hazard Adams
GEORGE RUSSELL (AE)	Richard M. Kain and James O'Brien
DION BOUCICAULT	Peter A. Tasch
THOMAS DAVIS	Eileen Ibarra
LOUIS MACNEICE	Christopher Armitage
PADRAIC COLUM	Charles Burgess
PEADAR O'DONNELL	Grattan Freyer
OLIVER ST. JOHN GOGARTY	J. B. Lyons
THOMAS KINSELLA	David Clark
SEAN O'FAOLAIN	Joseph Browne
F. R. HIGGINS	Timothy Brownlow

The Cup of Sand (Verse)
Bronze Woman (Verse)
A. E. Coppard: His Life and His Poetry . . .
The Wedding of Sir Gawain and Dame Ragnell (Translation)
Unimagined Rose (Verse)
"Only Necessity . . ." (Verse)
King Noggin (Children's Tale)
Selected Lyrics
The Elusive Stallion (Essays on Poetry, Art, and the Artist)
October Sheaf (Verse)
Handbook of English Grammar and Writing Conventions
Stephens, Yeats, and Other Irish Concerns
Prolegomena to the Study of Yeats's Poems
Prolegomena to the Study of Yeats's Plays
The Age of Yeats (Anthology)
Four Songs (Words & Music)
Owls' Watch (Anthology of Short Stories)
In . . . Luminous Wind (Essays on Yeats)
Quintet: Essays on Five American Women Poets
The Wild Queen (Novella)
Rushlight Heritage: Reflections on Selected Irish Short-Story Writers of the Yeatsian Era
Hound and Unicorn: Collected Verse—Lyrical, Narrative, and Dramatic
Carved in Findruine (Short Stories on Old Irish Themes)
Concise Introduction to Types of Literature in English
A Little Book of Strange Tales
Withdrawn in Gold (Essays on Stephens, Hodgson, and Dinesen)
Traditional Irish Literature and Its Backgrounds: A Brief Introduction (Revision of *The Shadow of the Three Queens*)
In Mountain Shadow (Novel)
Seumas O'Kelly: A Monograph
The Forgotten Birthday (Children's Tale)
Candlelight Rhymes for Early-to-Beds
Liadain and Curithir . . . (Irish Novella + Four Short Stories)
A Touch of Acid (Satiric Verse)
Advice to the Emotionally Perturbed (Parody)
Postscript to Hound and Unicorn (Verse)
Skeleton's Progress (Second PS to *Hound and Unicorn*)

DANIEL CORKERY

George Brandon Saul

Lewisburg
BUCKNELL UNIVERSITY PRESS

©1973 by Associated University Presses, Inc.

Associated University Presses, Inc.
Cranbury, New Jersey 08512

Library of Congress Cataloging in Publication Data

Saul, George Brandon, 1901–
    Daniel Corkery.

    (The Irish writers series)
    Bibliography: p.
    1. Corkery, Daniel, 1878–1964.
PR6005.065Z87   828'.9'1209   72-125298
    ISBN 0-8387-7754-6
    ISBN 0-8387-7699-X (pbk.)

Printed in the United States of America

Contents

7

Acknowledgments

Various people have aided me, directly or by suggestion, in assembling biographical data and facilitating work on this monograph, which was in large degree made possible by a grant from the University of Connecticut Research Foundation, and which is primarily concerned with Corkery's nontractarian creative work in English, the slight matter in Irish being passed by. I am most deeply indebted to my wife, who shared with me the tedious job of combing the highly miscellaneous and then-unclassified Corkery papers. After her, I must name especially Mr. Daniel O'Keefe, Librarian of University College, Cork, for kindly granting access to the papers in reference; Mr. Henchy, the enormously helpful Librarian of the National Library of Ireland; Miss Maureen Corkery, for both information and hospitality; Mrs. Ena Hendrick; and those particular friends of Corkery's, the sculptor Mr. Seamus Murphy, the late Mr. Seán Hendrick, and Mr. Liam Russell.

Chronology

(*N.B.:* Corkery's entire life was centered in Cork and the nearby countryside.)

1878: Born 14 February at 1, Gardiner's Hill, Cork; son of William and Mary (Barron) Corkery. Educated initially at Presentation Brothers Elementary School, Douglas St., Cork, where he taught for some years as a monitor.

1901: ". . . I became an enthusiast in the struggle to make the Irish language once more the vernacular of the country."

1906: Entered St. Patrick's College, Dublin, for a year's study, 5 September. Returned to Cork to resume work as a National Teacher in elementary schools until 1921; at some time during this period studied nights at the Crawford Municipal School of Art.

1908: Helped organize Cork Dramatic Society, for which he wrote his first plays; subsequently founder-member of the Munster Fine Arts Society.

1916: *A Munster Twilight.*

1917: *The Threshold of Quiet.*

1919: *The Labour Leader* produced by Abbey 30 September.

1920: *The Labour Leader* and *The Hounds of Banba* published. *The Yellow Bittern* produced by Abbey 4 May; *The Yellow Bittern and Other Plays* published.

1921: *I Bhreasail | A Book of Lyrics.*

1923-28: Clerical Assistant to County Cork "Inspector of Irish."

1925: *The Hidden Ireland.*

1928-31: "Irish Organizer" (as previously "itinerant" art teacher in various schools, afternoons and nights), County Cork Vocational School Educational Committee.

1929: *The Stormy Hills.*—M.A., with first class honors, National University of Ireland, for independent research on Synge and Anglo-Irish Literature.

1931: *Synge and Anglo-Irish Literature.*—Professor of English, University College, Cork.

1939: *Earth out of Earth.*—*Fohnam the Sculptor* produced by the Abbey 28 August.

1947: Retired from University College, Cork.

1948: Honorary D. Litt., National University of Ireland. Honored by testimonial issue of *An Siol.*

1950: *The Wager* . . . (Selective edition of short stories) .

1951-54: Member of Seanad Éireann, on nomination of Taoiseach.

1952: "Co-opted" for membership in The Arts Council.

1954: *The Fortunes of the Irish Language.*—One-man exhibition of paintings in Dublin. (Previous and later participation in group exhibitions of Munster Fine Arts Society in Cork, *e.g.,* in 1958.)

1964: Died 31 December at home of niece Maureen Corkery, 6 Victoria Terrace, Glenbrook, County Cork. Subsequent burial in St. Joseph's Cemetery, Cork.

Daniel Corkery

I

Daniel Corkery, one of the least justifiably neglected contributors to the Irish Renaissance, is an author whose quiet life, centered in Cork and its environs, stirred little publicity outside Ireland. (At home, some readers even suspected his surname to be a pseudonym indicative of the Cork and Kerry backgrounds of his writing!) Indeed, such knowledge as we have of his life may be summed up briefly, with the prefatory observation that Corkery was one whose courtesy and generosity, despite what a former pupil calls his "fierce and angry spirit . . . impatient with wrong thinking," left little but warm admiration to light the reminiscences of his friends. *Extreme* generosity, in fact, is the characteristic emphasized by the sculptor Seamus Murphy, his happily indebted former student, whose bust of him stands in the gallery of Cork's Crawford School of Art; and Diarmuid Murphy calls him "the gentlest, kindest gentleman I have ever known." True, he is also remembered as one who detested "smart Alecs"—the "clever" Dubliners. One suspects this may help explain Frank O'Connor's attribution to him of "a good deal of the

17

harshness and puritanism of the provincial intellectual," though one must grant that there are elements
even in Corkery's fiction that seem to justify O'Connor's feeling. Further, a letter of 20 May 1922 from the
Talbot Press indicates that his relations with his pub-
lisher could be crotchety and demanding, though any
experienced author could assume likely justification on
this score! Certainly "harshness and puritanism" are not
the characteristics suggested by the recollections of most
of Corkery's friends; indeed, he is remembered as one
who "could tell and enjoy a bawdy story," and as one
whose idealization of women drew the line at crediting
them with any brains.

In random testimony, one recalls the picture delin-
eated in personal correspondence by Mrs. Ena Hendrick, sister-in-law to Seán Hendrick, one of Corkery's
closest friends: "His large brown eyes set in a small,
round dark head, seemed to penetrate to one's very
soul; and even when he graciously saluted the passer-by,
one felt that those eyes were really looking into deeper,
more spiritual things, for he was a deeply religious
man." Lia Clarke, writing in the *Irish Press* for 25
August 1939, testifies: "I suppose Daniel Corkery is the
quietest man I ever met. But his is not the kind of
quietness that arises from indifference or lack of vital-
ity. It is . . . the quietude of one whose mind is turned
inward . . . those slightly surprised eyes lead one back
to repose. He has bright eyes . . . gentle manners . . .
he is very genuinely modest." And the diarist Joseph
Holloway, recording a visit to Dublin by Corkery on

29 July 1921, offers this description: "Corkery is small
in frame and delicate looking, and his right leg is short,
and, though he uses a big solid boot, he walks with
the limp of a cripple. [Close personal friends of Corkery's have assured me the damaged leg was his *left* one,
injured by an early—and presumably undiagnosed—
attack of poliomyelitis.] His head, like his body, is
small, but well-shaped, and he wears a moustache. He is
silent but observant . . . has a sweet, pleasing smile,
with just the slightest hint of cynicism shading off its
soothing quality." One may add, apropos of incidental
accomplishment, that he learned the cello and sang
baritone. Professor Breatnach, a former student of his,
asserts that "Sheer will-power alone helped him over-
come a stutter and the handicap of a maimed foot"; he
recalls the "limping figure with its balancing thrust of
shoulder, the head thrown back to the right side, the
candid scrutiny of the eyes in his perpetually serene
countenance, the face itself—fresh-featured and shiny
as the skin of an apple . . . the halting walk . . . that
voice which was oddly attractive despite its rather harsh
timbre." And to Francis Mac Manus, who remembers
him as "a medium-sized man, kind-faced . . . peering
sharply with bright glinting eyes through horn-rimmed
glasses," Corkery seemed "a prophet-patriarch": "I had
never met a mind like his outside books. It was a whole
country, populous, prolific, and yet full of great quiet
places into which he would suddenly withdraw."

In any event, the man in question was born 14 February 1878 at 1, Gardiner's Hill, on the northern edge

of Cork, coming paternally of five or six generations of carpenter-craftsmen, some of whose ability he might seem to have inherited, as suggested by the expertly fashioned, and finished, bookcases and "Morris chair with a detachable desk" (in O'Connor's phrase) which he constructed. (His brother William, and William's son, carried on the family tradition of carpentry.) His father, William Corkery, died early; his mother, Mary (née Barron) , who had been reared at sea, in her eighties. There were two brothers, the just-mentioned William and Edward, the latter of short span; and there was Mary, the "Sis" who was Corkery's devoted companion and housekeeper throughout life, and who survived him. With these may be appropriately recalled the maid "Kate," who, blind for thirty-five years, was cared for by Corkery and eventually buried in his grave. (The only woman whom rumor considered a romantic interest to Corkery died young of tuberculosis.)

Corkery, who grew up into a nonsmoking, nondrinking man, was educated initially by the Presentation Brothers at their elementary school in the South Monastery on Douglas Street, Cork. There he held a King's Scholarship and taught for some years as a monitor, thus, in the manner of the time, qualifying for later professional appointment (which, luckily for him, was not conditional on possession of an earned baccalaureate degree) . In early manhood, he joined the Gaelic League and began the study of Irish, becoming a veritable fanatic in his propagation of the language. ˙

Apparently, though, he did not attain high personal fluency in writing Irish, if one may trust the implications of such men as Diarmuid Murphy, who, writing in the *Capuchin Annual* for 1967, says (obviously forgetting "Clan Falvey") that "any of his plays that are in Irish were put there by Pádraig ó Domhnaill." Shortly after the turn of the century, too, Corkery was contributing to the early *Leader* over the pseudonym "Lee."

For over two decades Corkery labored as a National Teacher in elementary schools, including St. Francis B.N.S., off North Main Street, Cork, where he was appointed an assistant in October 1905, and to which he returned in 1907 after a hiatus for study at St. Patrick's College, Dublin. At St. Patrick's, whose first division course he entered 5 September 1906, he made a thoroughly good record, though he was graded only "Fair" in "Progress in Teaching" and "Good" in "English Composition"! About five years after returning to St. Francis, he moved to St. Patrick's National School, from which he resigned in 1921 after being refused the headmastership. It was here that he taught Seamus Murphy, fated to become with his encouragement a notable sculptor, and Michael O'Donovan, the eventually famous author "Frank O'Connor," who was in some degree to memorialize him in his autobiographies. Meanwhile he had by 1911 moved from 31 Barrack Street to 9 Ophelia Place ("The Lough"), from whence he transferred to 1 Auburn Villas, Ashburton, his domicile in 1917. It was at some undeter-

mined point during his elementary school teaching
(which O'Connor indicates was not free of either un-
ruffled temper or sly propaganda for the Irish language)
that he began studying at night at the Crawford School
of Art. Eventually he secured a cottage at Iniscarra, on
the Lee, for his painting, in which water color was his
preferred medium. Meanwhile, he had also been engag-
ing in other activities of a cultural nature.

II

On 1 November 1908, about the time the sculptor Joseph Higgins undertook the bust which O'Connor speaks of having seen in the Gardiner's Hill home and which now stands in University College, Cork, Corkery helped organize the Cork Dramatic Society. He served this Society as secretary and associate director during its approximately six years of flourishing. His own summary of this activity is included in his reminiscences of Con O'Leary in the University College, Cork *Record*, No. 34: "In 1908 Traolach Mac Suibhne [Terence MacSwiney], myself, and a few others, mostly teachers, and all Gaelic Leaguers, founded a dramatic movement in Cork. The Abbey Theatre, then at its best, was the inspiration. We, however, had our own views on the ideals of that theatre. Our aim was gradually to eliminate the play in English, replacing it by a play in Irish. We staged only such plays as had been written for us. They were mostly one-act plays, with an occasional one in three acts; and the supply was ample. We played and rehearsed in premises known as An Dún ["The Fort," in Queen Street], in the possession

23

of the Gaelic League, paying that body a very low rent. After five or six years 1916 was in the offing, and gradually An Dún became a hall for drilling in. Even our actors took to drilling. Somehow we dissolved." Incidentally, a subscription of five shillings admitted one to all performances for a year.

Corkery's connection with this organization led to his prentice work as a dramatist, most of which can be examined (mainly without great reward) among the manuscripts preserved in University College, Cork Library. Included are such efforts as *The Embers,* a three-acter and the Society's initial offering, 13 May 1909, later submitted pseudonymously to, and produced by, Radio Telefís Éireann; *The Eternal Longing,* a one-acter; and *The Woman of Three Cows,* a four-acter, whose manuscript is dated 3 October 1909. This last is a study in pride and its downfall, with the possibilities inherent in its theme negated by verboseness and a clumsily protracted ending, as well as by the difficulty of believing the mother would not recognize her son in the decayed priest come home to die.

Also among these prentice plays is *The Hermit and the King* (> "King and Hermit," published in *The Yellow Bittern and Other Plays*), a one-acter of 2 December 1909, praised in *The Leader* for 14 January 1911, which calls Corkery the "chief playwright of the Dun." And there are several others. *The Onus of Ownership,* a one-act comedy in sixty manuscript pages and not really a bad one, though somewhat loosely structured, is concerned with a landlord's troubles with female tenants, and was produced 19 April 1911. *The Epilogue,* 19 May 1911, is an unexciting script dealing with the disillusionment of a stranded dramatic company. Finally, there is the four-act *Israel's Incense,* dated 2 December 1912 in a program of the Cork Opera House and favorably reviewed the next day by the *Free Press* and the Cork *Constitution,* though Moirin Chavasse has remarked that "Corkery's long play was badly received, being . . . over the heads of the audience" (*Terence MacSwiney*—Dublin: Clonmore and Reynolds Ltd.; London: Burns and Oates Ltd., 1961, p. 29). Of this last play, which eventually became *Fohnam the Sculptor,* at least four typescripts exist, and dating shows that Corkery was still working on it in 1935.

In 1912 Corkery began his novel, *The Threshold of Quiet,* though it was not published until 1917. Meanwhile he was also writing short stories, and a collection of these, *A Munster Twilight,* became in 1916 his first published book, as well as (in 1917) the first of his American issues. The approval of reviewers was emphatic and widespread—prophetic, indeed, of the reception generally to be accorded his fiction. Acclaim ranged from Katharine Tynan's perceptive review in *Studies* (6: 138–39), which frankly—and rightly—ascribed genius to the author, to the recognition of verisimilitude and novelty in a wide spectrum of Irish, Scots, and English notices.

Indeed, it would be almost impossible to overpraise this charming, quiet, and unaffected book, which contains a dozen miscellaneous stories and a loose sequence

entitled "The Cobbler's Den."* The most memorable
tale is "The Ploughing of Leaca-na-Naomh" (entitled
"The Ploughing of the Leaca" in *The Wager* . . .).
This account of the tragedy—and lifelong entailment
thereto—that resulted from a farmer's forcing a fool by
repeated suggestion to plough the ancient burial
ground of the saints touches greatness. Despite an awk-
ward beginning, its fusion of wildness of substance with
quietness of telling produces both epic tension and
epic picture. The result is a haunting, unforgettable
experience.

Certain other tales in *A Munster Twilight* are almost
equally memorable. A case in point is the semi-mystical
"The Cry," in which Old Larry will not, despite the
temptation of American gold, forsake the lonely road
of the anonymous dead man to whose cairn generations
of passers-by have contributed stones and prayers. With
it stand preeminently such tales as "The Return,"
"Storm-Struck," "The Spanceled," and "Solace." The
first concerns a sailor, Jim Daunt, and his drowning
by his ship after a night ashore and the possible murder
of a shipmate. The second records the tragedy of John
Donovan, who returns blinded from the Montana cop-
per mine where he was trying to earn enough to marry
Kitty Regan, only to find her married. The third is
concerned with the circumvention of a will that would
have bound a widow intolerably. The last—racy of the
breed it presents—tells how an eighteenth-century poet,

---

*Discussion of this volume, as also of subsequent collections of short
stories, draws heavily on the writer's *Rushlight Heritage*.

facing eviction, makes a poem and then sacrifices his only cow for a final celebration with local fellow-poets!

As I have said elsewhere, *A Munster Twilight* is written in a natural, conversational style. Quite without the smell of the lamp, it is a first collection any autnor might take pride in: a book curiously prophetic in tone of the sort of thing Frank O'Connor was later to do even more beautifully. The author's way of moralizing a situation, or *seeming to threaten to do so*, is the only mildly unpleasant thing about it.

On 9 July 1917 the Talbot Press sent Corkery first galleys of *The Threshold of Quiet*. Appearance of the book later in the year (it had to wait until 1933 for an Irish translation to be published in Dublin) occasioned another chorus of wide approval, with the Belfast *Irish News* (3 November 1917) crowning the author Ireland's "most notable writer of fiction" and Peter Mc-Brien (*Studies*, December 1917) labeling the volume "the finest Irish novel that has ever been published." Some disapproval there was (perhaps feared in anticipation by Ernest Boyd, who after reading and approving the manuscript for the Talbot Press urged Corkery in a personal letter to "delete the occasional redundancies, and tighten up the threads," but who certainly backed the book in a long review in *The Freeman*, 20 October 1917). An anonymous reviewer in *Irish Life* (16 November 1917) confessed "some rather undefined feeling of disappointment" because while "tragedy there must be in life . . . it is only when it is inevitable that it becomes impressive." And *The New Age* (11 September 1918) remarked drily, "Cork seems

to be a place where literally nothing happens and *The
Threshold of Quiet* records the fact in 300 pages of
miserable musings." Against this derogation must be
recalled the support of such periodicals as the London
Times Literary Supplement, the Manchester *Guardian,*
and the *Athenaeum;* the protest of Hugh Walpole
(*Land and Water,* 7 March 1918) against what he
counted neglect and lack of appreciation; and the fact
that the book has retained its champions for almost
half a century. Even Seán O'Faoláin counts it "one of
the best Irish novels ever written" and better than any
of his own. And Ernest Boyd asserts roundly (*Ireland's
Literary Renaissance,* edn. 1922, p. 397) , "Daniel Corkery and James Joyce have brought the Irish novel back
into literature."

In a little essay, "The Spirit of Victory," published
in *The Ship* ("A Cork Republican Monthly") , 10
June 1922, Corkery remarks that "the thoughtful spirit
that creates enduring works . . . is not blatant nor loud-
voiced, but timid; except indeed when it is withdrawn
within the realms of thought, whose unwritten laws it
understands and obeys." Perhaps it is a suggestion of
timidity that makes *The Threshold of Quiet* for the
present commentator unexciting and gives it the
"middle-aged" tenor which O'Faoláin ascribes to it
even as he approves it.

Such action as occurs takes place mainly between
Martin Cloyne's home on "the Lough," south of Cork
(was there subtle significance in Corkery's signing
himself "Martin Cloyne" in a book sent O'Connor
when the latter was jailed by the Free State soldiers?) ,

and Lily Bresnan's, Fair Hill, on a rise to the north of the city.

We are introduced to several friends of Frank Bresnan, a young commercial traveler just drowned in the Lee: Martin, Ned Connell, a certain "Ring," and Stevie Galvin, lover of Minnie Ryan, but estranged from her since the quarrel with his younger brother, Phil, which sent the latter to sea. There follows Frank's wake, at which Martin's inclination toward Lily—and hers toward him—is intimated, and old John Bresnan's deprecatory attitude toward Finnbar, his younger son, becomes evident. Then comes a verbose, almost maundering account of humdrum darkened by religious morbidity and only slightly sharpened by the tragic events of John Bresnan's sudden pneumonia, leading to quick death, and Phil Galvin's loss in his hurricane-wrecked ship off Ballymachus before his conscience-stricken brother can welcome him home in reconciliation. Events in general are curiously colorless and limply presented. Ned Connell, twice sacked from the same job, takes a position with Martin's uncle in New York. Finnbar, vacillating between the priesthood and the sea, chooses the latter. The supposedly exemplary Frank Bresnan is revealed as a suicide after getting engaged to " 'a good, simple, *stupid* girl' "; Stevie's quarrel with Phil is shown as rooted in the latter's effort to make love to Minnie Ryan; Lily, urged on by her priest, who says he is acting at the request of the dead Frank, ends in a convent even though she has shown no strong inclination toward a vocation and has even changed her confessor temporarily to obviate embarrassment. (We are told she "leant greatly to the belief, common amongst Irish Catholics, that the right course in matters affecting the soul is that which does not seem to square exactly with what we call reason.") Her putative, shilly-shallying lover Martin piously accepts the situation, feeling that Kilvirra, the location of the convent, is now "filled with a light—a clear light that would shine for ever." Obviously, he is not broken-hearted as this book of some three hundred pages dissolves in sentimentality: perhaps he lacks blood enough to be so.

Although it has been suggested that this novel may be Corkery's best work, the writer can only say, regretfully, that he must share the opinion of *The New Age*. His first reading left him mainly with quickly evanescent impressions of locale, while his second—years later—was sheer struggle. Corkery's characters, obviously fearful of their own thought whenever they feel it may threaten to counter Roman Catholic doctrine, are simply tedious. The whole affair suggests the expanded reflection of a neurosis; in long stretches it becomes almost as tiresome as the "psychological" meanderings of George Moore. The "readings of life" are homely and unmemorable: compare, "We are always proud of what we fancy ourselves overdoing!" The prose—occasionally marred by a dangling construction or a mischosen tense—is competent but unexciting, abusive of the adjective *wild,* and spattered with unnecessary exclamation points. And the author's profundity and perspicacity may be judged from his assertion that "not myriad-minded men are wanted" in America. To top it all, there is a sense of implied moralization going hand in hand with an effort to dramatize sentimentality (Martin's lips, *e.g.,* are "as tender-looking as a nun's"!). It is natural that Corkery's genuine, if parochial, piety should have colored his underlying thought; it is sad that it should have spanceled as frequently as it did the natural reflections and impulses of his characters. No wonder that his title should have emerged from Thoreau's "The mass of men lead lives of quiet desperation," though he manages to suggest here more quiet than desperation. Perhaps saddest of all, the book intimates what subsequent writing establishes: Corkery's inability, whatever his other unquestionable gifts, to rise to a love story.

On 30 September 1919 *The Labour Leader,* a three-act play dedicated to Corkery's old friend Con O'Leary and in O'Faoláin's opinion "evidently suggested by . . . Jim Larkin," was introduced by Lennox Robinson at the Abbey with a notable cast. Though it appears to have been cordially received by the audience, and *Studies* (December 1920) counts it "a very good play," approving its character-drawing and dialogue (while questioning the dramatic effectiveness of the boxing match in the last act), one of the few available reviews claims that Corkery "falters noticeably" because he "does not understand" the "rugged ways" of the laborers and "there is an interminable amount of talk, a little of it entertaining, but most of it tiresome and unnecessary." And another review calls it "interesting, but never convincing," with too much talk, wrangling "between the forces of Labour itself," and an unresolved question for the audience: "What was the strike all about—what was the issue?" Concerned as it is with an almost maudlin progression of events sparked by the railroaders' not having joined in the Cork quaymen's six-week-old strike, the play is tractarian in its motivating concept. But it is unredeemed dramatically by the momentary excitement of the fighting that precipitates its turning point—the intimation that the railroaders will support the strike. Certainly it is a work properly characterized by Catharine Rynne as "more remarkable for its subject matter than its artistic merit." Perhaps, as suggested in *The Leader* (27 November 1920) , it is "made up of interests that Apollo couldn't easily string his lyre to, try with all his might!" Nevertheless, it was published in 1920, with a sarcastic preface obviously implying a jab at Shaw.

Meanwhile Corkery had been active as a leading member of the "Twenty Club," which is remembered as having met each Sunday in Cork and having published AN LA until it was suppressed by the British Military Authority (Dublin Castle) . (Cf. *Irish Independent,* 1 January 1965.) Thereafter he became one of the founding members of the Munster Fine Arts Society, successor to the extinguished club.

The year in which *The Labour Leader* was published must have been one of Corkery's most exciting. On 4 May *The Yellow Bittern* was produced by the Abbey; later in the year it became the title piece of a volume of three plays (one of which, "Clan Falvey," was in an Irish translation by Seán Tóibín entitled "Ó Fáilbhe Mór" produced by Corkery and the St.

Finnbarr Gaelic Leaguers in the "Grianan," Cork, 4
April 1919, with Seán O'Faoláin in the title role, and
published in Dublin in 1920). According to O'Connor
(*A Short History of Irish Literature,* p. 170), Yeats
had accepted *The Yellow Bittern* (first performed by
the Munster Players at Father Matthew's Hall, Cork,
10 May 1917) "as part of the Abbey canon" because,
like many of his own pieces, it was a "miracle"; and
the play won a "salute" for Corkery in *The Day* (Cork,
Midsummer 1917), while the book in which it appeared was acknowledged by *The Leader* (27 November
1920) to be "made of the stuff that poetry is made of."
Studies, in turn, noted (December 1920) "the atmosphere of mysticism" pervading the volume, while
counting the title piece "easily the best."

The judgment is sound, although all three inclusions
in *The Yellow Bittern and Other Plays* are companion-
able in quality; and this is the book that really establishes Corkery as a dramatist. That it has long been
out of print implies a comment on the lack of perspicacity in commercial publishing. Of its trio of one-
acters, "King and Hermit" (in its original form, said
to have been hurriedly written to fill out a program
of the Cork Dramatic Society in 1909) is laid in a wood
in "early Christian Ireland." Led by a visionary fawn
while out hunting, the aged King Manus comes with
three courtiers to the forest hut of the old hermit
Colman, whose gilly is the boy Rory. Won by the
hermit's praise of peace, he resigns his crown, thereafter recognizing and becoming reconciled with Colman, who is really his brother, driven away in youth

by his cruelty. This is a quiet, charming, gentle piece, perhaps more suggestive of a short story than of a play, but—like its fellows—genuinely touching; perhaps it might be best described as essentially a dramatic idyl. Of its fellows, "Clan Falvey" is laid in an early eighteenth-century peasant's hut. Old Sean O'Falvey has—to the bitter disgust of his son Hugh—bartered the family's "hoardings," instead of using them to repair the dykes of the rising river threatening their fields, for a manuscript "poem-book" from which he hopes to reconstruct his ancient lineage. When a shanachie finally unravels the "secret" poetry of the manuscript, O'Falvey's pride of ancestry is confirmed—but at ultimate cost of dispossession of what little remains to him and his two sons. And when he falls in the wind, en route to "the Brehon stone," he is carried to his bed, doomed to recover from his injuries but to face assured misery. And here Corkery has provided a play moving, poetic, and powerful on every score.

The title play, in H. de Blacam's broad summary (*Gentle Ireland,* p. 146) , retells "the death-story of poor Cathal Buidhe . . . ne'er-do-well Northern poet . . . succored at death by Our Lady, as fable says, because he had made a song of praise for Her. . . ." We are introduced to two old men, Shawn MacDonnell and Hugh MacAleenan, arguing the merits of the Ulster song "An Bunan Bwee" ("The Yellow Bittern") and a Munster song, "Gile na Gile." Shawn backs the former, ascribed to a broken and once-disreputable poet, Cahal Bwee, who in the song compares himself to the harmless yellow bird, though the priests had

cursed him and any house offering him hospitality.
After Shawn has gone to lie down to recall the words
of "An Bunan Bwee" completely, old Cahal appears,
feverish and demanding rest, but is refused by Shawn's
married daughter Nora and Hugh, though the former
quickly repents. They watch Cahal going, unrecog-
nized, into the neighboring Gallaghers'. Nora Gallagher
runs for the priest while her mother, Sheela, comes to
Nora and Hugh—and learns who her sick guest is.
Meanwhile Cahal is writing his "Song of Repentance"
on a wall with burnt sticks. Then the priest appears,
come from the Gallagher house, to ask "what woman
was it welcomed" him there. Told that no woman was,
to their knowledge, in the house, he describes her and
says the place was candle-lit and ready for him and that
she took Cahal's hands after the sacrament preceding
his death-agony. The frightened priest and the others
are kneeling to pray when old Shawn comes from his
room, triumphantly quoting the rest of Cahal's drink-
ing song. Told by the priest of Cahal's death with his
soul "at peace," Shawn opens the door to go to the
Gallagher house, but is sent to his knees by the Virgin
Mary passing by in a great light. The others also make
obeisance and pray to her. O'Connor was quite right
in recognizing the play as a "miracle" in type: it is,
indeed, a very gentle one, with all the finest qualities
of its kind.

To 1920 belongs also *The Hounds of Banba,* though
the manuscript was conceivably ready two years earlier.
This set of stories, issued in both Ireland and America,
though the American edition followed the Irish by

two years, brought a few disapproving responses (and a letter of 30 August 1920 indicates that the chairman of the Talbot Press did not count the work up to the standard of *A Munster Twilight*), but also a large number of critical, and sometimes patently extravagant, endorsements. Mary Colum, Rose Macaulay, Susan Mitchell, and Katharine Tynan are representative of the approving Irish and English voices; American reviewers, in general, were favorable. And on 12 January 1921 the Talbot Press was able to report steady, if slow, sales in Ireland, though "the English sale" was "practically nil."

Actually, *The Hounds of Banba* ("Banba," of course, represents Ireland, symbolized in the figure of a reputed ancient queen of the *Tuatha Dé Danann*) is Corkery's lamest set of tales, though his personal opinion of them is doubtless suggested by the fact that he chose three of them for his selective volume, *The Wager*. Presented as reflections of the experiences of one engaged as an organizer of "Volunteers" (the "hounds" are revolutionaries), and interesting as a memorialization of guerrilla activities by a people operating out of an understandable historical hatred of the English, these nine stories reach complete bathos in "A Bye-Product," wherein a boorish half-wit is supposed to reach a sort of sanctification through participating in the revolutionary movement. All in all, the air of strain in the recording and of juvenility in some of the sentiments suggests that we have here a series of uneven efforts at writing heroic history episodically. As an anonymous reviewer remarked, "Mr. Corkery is rhetorical, he tells a story as if he were making a speech; but what might excite an audience of partisans is dull in cold print. He forgets that in a story one should relate events that arouse emotions rather than vent the emotions . . . of the author. . . ." Corkery's only additional publication in 1920 was apparently his December tribute in *Studies* to Terence MacSwiney, old friend, associate in early dramatic productions, fellow language-enthusiast, and erstwhile Lord Mayor of Cork, who had died on hunger strike in Brixton Prison on 25 October.

In 1921 came *I Bhreasail*, containing some verse presumably dating back to the days of the Cork Dramatic Society (to judge from the letterhead of the manuscript containing a draft of "Mother and Son"). Reviews appear to have been fewer than usual for a Corkery volume: I found about a dozen—again, almost uniformly favorable in tenor. But sales appear to have been disappointing: only six copies of the English edition between 1922 and 1926. (In paying the royalty of 1/6, Mathews & Marrot proposed in a letter of 1 January 1926 sending "25 copies in lieu of further royalties.") And Katharine Tynan's review (*Studies*, May 1922) seems to veil a certain disappointment in its conclusion: "Mr. Corkery's verse in this book shows no signs of competing with his prose; but it is individual, it has moments of beauty; and there is always interest in looking into the mind of a poet, even if his highest expression lies in prose." It may be significant that Padraic Colum chose from this volume only one lyric ("No Miracle") for his *Anthology of Irish Verse,* and that Farren passes by the author completely in his *Course of Irish Verse in English.*

I Bhreasail ("Isle of the Blessed," one of various designations of the Gaelic paradise), dedicated to Professor Stockley (Corkery's predecessor at University College, Cork) and his wife, is a 76-page book divided into "Men and Women" (fourteen pieces), "Miscellaneous" (eighteen), "Sonnets" (ten), and "Lute Songs" (seven). Its matter is readable, very personal for the most part, and pleasantly traditional without being imitative. Nor is it derivative except for an implied minor debt to Yeats in "the cloud of hair" ("Of One Who Is Dead") and for the epithet "wine-dark" ("Storm"), which may have arrived from Homer either directly or by way of Mangan, and which may just conceivably have been plucked from this volume by Yeats. The opening group of poems is the most noteworthy; the third group is competent, commonplace, and essentially rhetorical; the final group is the most graceful, but is easily forgotten, even though here love's kiss unveils for the poet "The peaks of I Bhreasail purple and dim!"

This is a very Irish book, reflecting a racial inclination to apostrophe; a book obviously, and happily, indebted to a ballad tradition and nourished by rural background, with much to testify that to Corkery Ireland was always a land whose "every field" was "as a verse of high enduring song." It contains several memorials to the martyrs of the Easter Rising and an elegy—"In Memoriam"—for a personally unknown man

lost on the *Titanic* which in some degree fails as elegiac
verse too frequently does, even when produced by a
Milton or a Yeats, being suggestive of sympathetic
rhetoric rather than heartbreak. There is a tribute "To
Raftery," a lament "From the Irish" by a girl forsaken
by her lover, a greeting to Pat Higgins (brother of the
sculptor Joseph) upon his release from political incar-
ceration in a British jail. There is restrained poetic
wildness, as in "No Miracle," where Felimid, having
ruined his wife's beauty by a blow, plucks out his eyes
in consequence. Very rarely, the verse becomes senti-
mentally silly, as in "Chanty," or coyly homely, as
when a bird, in "Storm," is fancied to be "yearning
to go / Ashrink and ahide in her nest. . . ." (And those
abuses of the proclitic—"ahide," "adown," "adream,"
"a-tiptoe," "a-shout," etc.—do become tiresome.)

Technically faultless the book is not: one thinks of
flawed metre in the fifth stanza of the opening lyric,
as also in "Love Triumphant"; of mismanaged accent,
as in "The Free Day"; of lapses into flat prose, as in
"There's so much to do the whole day long." Further,
too much of the verse (like that of many readable
poets) simply lacks poetic charge: one reads, but seldom
with impulse to reread; and the sentimentalist too
often seems hiding around the corner, as when April
is implored to "Come in and live among us men, / A
wild bird in our slavery." And occasionally (as often
in his short stories) the poet suggests a verging toward
moralization (cf. "Love's Motley"). Nor do poems
always end so well as their openings promise.

Why, then, does one value possession of this—in a

manner of speaking—shy book? Perhaps because of a
curious but undeniable charm; because, in Colum's
phrase, of its suggestion of "the earth-smell out of the
earth" (and pieces like "The Peasant" remind us of
Colum's *Wild Earth*); and because it is imbued with
gentle love of country and sympathy with racial kind.
Just incidentally, it may be added that a variant of the
first stanza of "Chanty" may be found in the "Prelude"
to *Fohnam the Sculptor.*

On 24 June 1921 Corkery was appointed a sort of
"itinerant" teacher of art in various Cork schools, working afternoons and nights, and during the twenties he
also gave summer refresher courses in literature and
drama for teacher-employees of the County Vocational
School Educational Committee. In 1922 he issued
pseudonymously the pamphlet *Rebel Songs,* dedicated
to Erskine Childers. This pretends to be nothing more
than its title suggests. The tone is intimated by "we've
failed, though we were right." Nonsupport of the rebels
is deplored, though eventual victory, however indefi-
nitely ahead, is projected. Even the priest who minis-
ters to the rebels is "As never before, a priest." And
occasionally imagination really flares, as in the metri-
cally and grammatically flawed "The Retreat from
Limerick," in which the soldiers are accompanied by
visionary figures and the ghosts of Sarsfield's army.
Here and there a compromise line seems to have been
dictated by metrical exigency as much as by anything
else, but by and large the verses are well beyond patriotic manufactures in poetic quality, though the ac-
knowledgment unfortunately supports no significant

claim. What might suggest Corkery's authorship were that unknown is a certain sensed gentleness and sadness of spirit, an intimacy with countryside and country folk, and the occasional use of a favorite adjective, "wild." And the intellectual rebel is evident enough:

> The dead do not betray us, whatever's preached or said
> From altar cross or market cross for love of peace or gain.

On 25 January 1923 Corkery became clerical assistant to the County Cork "Inspector of Irish," continuing in this appointment until his resignation on 1 October 1928. In April of 1924 he published the play "Resurrection" in the *Theatre Arts Monthly* (America). In its apparently much later (?1942), but undated, Talbot Press pamphlet edition, there is a note (not completely accurate in detail) saying it was written in 1918, but that the authorities in Dublin Castle had refused permission to publish. That Corkery thought well of it seems implied by the fact that he printed it *twice* in the *Capuchin Annual* (1930 and 1936); that the Castle would have been justified if it could have based its position on aesthetic grounds is a frivolously permissible rumination.

The play, laid in the ex-Fenian Terence Cantwell's farmhouse, "on the borders of Dublin County," early Easter Tuesday, 1916, has to do with the initially vacillatory old man's "resurrection" of the fighting and sacrificial spirit within himself after his wounded son Michael comes home to die and his other son, Shaun, leaves for apparently assured death. Bathos could conceivably not go much farther than when Terence, after initially suspecting Michael of being a traitor but learning that he has been wounded, crows, "He's wounded? Glory be to the Father, the Son, and the Holy Ghost"; or than when his only worry at his other son's departure is whether he can trust the boy to face his executioners with unbandaged eyes, and his boast is "There'll be no fear in this house any longer." What a reading of fatherhood—and what a contrast to, say, Yeats's *Cathleen Ni Houlihan* in the achievement of patriotic drama!

Without, however legitimately, deploring abuse of religious connotations in the title, one can only regret this bit of propagandistic mawkishness. *Resurrection* is a piece of childish and almost incredible heroizing (cf. *The Hounds of Banba*). The father's initial suspicion of Michael is overdone, and the whole piece is suggestive of semi-dramatic conversation rather than of convincing progression and integration. Take away the patriotic fueling and the jibes at past English cruelty, and the thing has not even tenuous justification.

In 1925 Corkery issued *The Hidden Ireland,* which he considered his most important book. It appears to have been commercially his most successful, and it remains clearly one of his most controversial. O'Faoláin calls it (*Dublin Magazine,* April-June 1936) "a history, in effect, of 18th Century Ireland from the point of view of the penalised underdog"; O'Connor (*Short History* . . . , p. 114) labels it "a very lyrical and wrongheaded book" about "a poetry that, like the people who wrote it, was being steadily degraded socially." Proponents of the book, which reached its third impression in 1941, dismiss such disparagement as the opinion of "Corkery's gluggers" (i.e., rotten eggs), which fact makes adverse judgment hazardous still. Nevertheless, provincial chauvinism has rarely exceeded the extravagance of some champions of this book: for example, that of A. de Blacam, who calls it "majestic," and that of H. de Blacam in *Gentle Ireland* when he writes (p. 147): "a spacious study . . . has given a new impulse to Irish letters. . . . Every new Irish writer who counts . . . acknowledges himself indebted to this wonderful book . . . a grand monument of prose—a great, grave, devout book . . . one of the biggest things done in our age in any land . . . it makes Corkery the greatest of our realists. . . ." The best answer to which, as also the best criticism of the book, may be Cullen's calmly dispassionate "The Hidden Ireland: Re-assessment of a Concept," in *Studia Hibernica,* No. 9 (1969), obnoxious though it appear to be to some of Corkery's old friends.

Actually a work in which chauvinism amounts to militant sentimentality, the book is subtitled "A Study of Gaelic Munster in the Eighteenth Century," though, as chapter 6 admits, the essential concern is really only with southwestern Munster; and the recurrent whipping boys are the historian Lecky (for ignoring the "literature" of the century) and the "novelists." By chapter 3, Corkery is ruminating on the Bardic Schools (generally thought to have persisted into the eighteenth century only in Scotland); by chapter 4, he achieves such a critical novelty as "Prose, as opposed to poetry, concerns itself with the civic life of man . . ." while building toward a rhapsody on the products of the "Courts of Poetry" (eventually reduced to assembling in taverns). The provincialism of these "courts" he glosses over by pretension for the sake of their "style": really, because of the simple fact that the verse is in Irish and reflects, he feels, racial tradition. And he develops a veritable froth of enthusiasm over the *aisling*, or "vision poem" (after all, "the vision the poet always sees is the spirit of Ireland as a majestic and radiant maiden"), launching himself on fantastic accounts of how peasant audiences *conceivably* responded to it.

By the time he gets to discussing his "poets" in detail, Corkery has actually identified Egan O'Rahilly as the "Dante of Munster," imagining that if some of his elegies were "chanted . . . one's spirit might fail before them, as before certain movements in Beethoven's symphonies"! But, unsurprisingly, he allows the audacious Merriman only about twenty pages, as compared with over twice as many granted Owen Roe O'Sullivan.

This book, with its verbose marshaling of defective scholarship and more-than-questionable critical and aesthetic judgment, has been for unbiased readers convincingly enough (and by no means viciously) disposed of on historical and factual grounds in Cullen's previously mentioned study. As O'Faoláin remarks (*Dublin Magazine*, April–June 1936), "It is a biggish book and it would take a bigger book to dispel the illusion of veracity it creates, for its arrangements of facts, and of half-facts, and of pious beliefs, by a man with an inadequate knowledge of Irish history, is tendencious in the extreme." As simple writing, it is marked by the inflation and exaltation of the enthusiast; it is repetitious; its fanciful reconstructions of biographical and general conditions involve many such betraying self-protections as "would very likely," "may, indeed, have been," "it is only fitting to imagine," and the like. Its sentimental "appreciations" of the verses frequently quoted both in Irish and in translation are as naïve as some of Douglas Hyde's, though more extravagant; and of course it considers many "poets" whose verse has at best only historical or sociological relevance instead of genuinely poetic quality. Even its occasional patches of charm are clouded by an emotionalism constantly running off into the verbose.

Between August 1925 and August 1927, Corkery published several short stories in *Columbia* (New Haven, Connecticut). From 1928 to 1931, he served as "Irish Organizer" for the County Cork Vocational School Educational Committee. Thereafter he moved to Ballygroman, Ovens, County Cork, where he remained until 1948. In 1929 he published another remarkable collection of short stories, *The Stormy Hills* (which included from *Columbia* "The Wager" and "The Eyes of the Dead"), and received an M.A., with first class honors, from the National University of Ireland for independent research on Synge and Anglo-Irish literature. On 10 April of the same year, D. Murphy's "A Desecration," based on Corkery's "The Ploughing of the Leaca," was produced by the St. Aidan Players at the Father Mathew Feis; a typescript is included in the Corkery papers at University College, Cork.

The Stormy Hills proved, most deservedly, another

critically well-received volume, and on 5 October 1929
Cape wrote to inform Corkery of "advance" orders for
over two hundred copies. Two of the most thoughtful reviews appeared in the Melbourne *Advocate* (26 December 1929) and the London *Times Literary Supplement* (4 November 1929). The former praised
Corkery's art in terms that seem just for all of his best
tales: "He is a realist in the best sense"—one who, un-
like certain fellow Irishmen, does not pretend "that the
dunghill is all the landscape"; who writes with sensitivity to poetry and beauty and out of a great "spiritual
endowment of sympathy." The *Times Literary Supplement*, with quiet rationality, noted that "Synge dis-
covered the larger rhythms of Irish idiomatic speech;
Mr. Corkery has developed the inward modulation
and quieter cadence of idiom: his style and suoject
express one another." Incidentally, the *Daily News* (12
March 1929) had the acuteness to recognize Corkery's
"rare power in giving a faint hint of the supernatural,
of the awesome, to stories which are ostensibly plain
narrative."

Indeed, *The Stormy Hills* is a remarkable collection
of exceptional, in several cases superlative, tales, in
which the recurrent place name is Youghal. Character
is rich in variety and presented with great subtlety of
implication; colloquialism and local idiom are admi-
rably handled. Only four of these fourteen stories seem
lesser things: "The Priest" (suggestive of sociology
rather than fiction), "Nightfall," "The Wandering
Spring," and "The Awakening," though Corkery chose
it for his selective volume. Of the rest I can say no

better than I already have in *Rushlight Heritage*: they
"touch quivering life at every point, and the mood is
almost invariably tragic. Corkery knows that 'truly we
walk darkling,' and his voice proves worthy of 'a land
where memory is steeped in the heroic.' Even his poor
must speak their passionate conviction. . . . And the
ancient plaint of kind, in whatever key, finds always a
sympathetic response in this author's heart.

"So we read of ancient Tadhg Kinnane, 'The Emp-
tied Sack' after he learns that his daughter has long
since drowned with the sea captain with whom she
eloped forty years before; of the drunken aristocrat and
his proud jockey in 'The Wager'; of the disgraced and
horsewhipped widower of 'The Ruining of Droma-
currig'; of the aged and blind tenement paralytic in 'A
Looter of the Hills' whose simple-minded son borrows
horse and cart without asking permission in order to
take her to visit the countryside of her childhood
once more before the death which leaves him melan-
choly . . . ; of the little shoemaker and the huge stone-
breaker who are 'The Rivals,' admittedly equal in
storytelling (the cobbler eventually left brooding on
how some day to win for himself a burial heroically
equal to that of his competitor!) ; and of many another.
More than once, in these folk, we recognize the characteristic Irish lust for land. But in the end, we may
conceivably find ourselves most haunted by 'The
Stones,' that unusual tale of a superstition to the effect
that those foredoomed to die were sometimes to be seen
in effigy in a remote place of stones, and of the tragic
results this superstition entailed.

"Being keenly responsive to the uncontrollable elements and malign influences in nature, Corkery is never better than in his scenes of wild country or of the sea by night; he writes of these with a restraint whose simplicity is at times almost epic ('it was as if a cromlech were marching out before them'), though it can be subtle as the perceptions of a musician. And to reenforce this ability, he possesses a faculty for somehow suggesting sculpture—not merely painting—where appropriate to his scenes ('a shaft of moonlight caught him, head and face. One would think a sword had struck him!'). One could ask little more of a volume of short stories than *The Stormy Hills* provides."

III

The unmixed cordiality which greeted *The Stormy Hills* was not prophetic of the reception accorded Corkery's next book, *Synge and Anglo-Irish Literature*, published in 1931, the year in which he resigned (1 October) as "Irish Organizer" and accepted the professorship in English at University College, Cork, to which he had been appointed, if common rumor may be credited, despite some vigorous opposition. In this position he is reported to have been unhappy, faced as he was by unprepared students off whose foreheads, he said, ideas merely bounced, though his niece, Maureen Corkery, has quoted him as saying "I've never been bored in my life." A former student of his, himself now a university professor, has characterized him conversationally as not a brilliant lecturer, but the sort who occasionally dropped nourishing ideas in his selective disquisitions. Nevertheless, the *Irish Times*, in its obituary, claims "it is rather as a tutor that he will best be remembered by his students and contemporaries. His provocative and challenging method of tuition . . . drew from and developed in his students, qualities and

ingenuity which otherwise would have been dormant
unless unfolded at a later period."—But to return to
Synge and Anglo-Irish Literature.

The book, of course, had its champions: Hugh de
Blacam (*Spectator,* 18 July 1931), hardly to be accused
of understatement, even asserted Shakespeare, Cervan-
tes, and Dante would have shared Corkery's view! The
Irish Independent credited it with "the authentic note
of greatness"; even the *New York Times, John o' London's Weekly,* the Manchester *Guardian,* and the *Fort-
nightly Review* lined up in approval. But the *Irish
Times* and *Universe* did not; and the author's fellow-
Corkman, P. S. O'Hegarty (cf. *Dublin Magazine,* Jan.-
Mar. 1932), came out devastatingly against it, blasting
its "general theory . . . in a nutshell, that only an Irish
Catholic Nationalist can write Irish literature," and
only, at that, if he is writing out of " 'three great forces
. . . (1) The Religious Consciousness of the People;
(2) Irish Nationalism; and (3) The Land.' " O'Hegarty pulled no punches: Corkery's theory, he asserted,
"is wrong-headed and damnable. It is carrying bigotry
and intolerance into literature. It is a denial of the
Irish Nation. It is prejudiced and, in the real sense,
ignorant." And he added that the Irish Nation was
made up of "all the people of this Island, Catholic and
non-Catholic, Gael and Sean-ghall, native and 'ascendancy,' " with Corkery seemingly unable to understand
that people write "to express themselves," not to serve
religion, race, or nationality; and must be judged "by
their workmanship." In time, Frank O'Connor (cf.
"Synge" in *The Irish Theatre*) was to give Corkery's

ideas sarcastic mauling, and Professor Tindall (*Forces in Modern British Literature* . . . , New York: Knopf, 1947, p. 83 n. 18) was to dismiss the book as "a plea for intolerant nationalism." Its substance had, however, won Corkery his M.A., and doubtless reenforced his propagandizing for the Irish language and the Gaelic League during his professorship and in his broadcasting stance during the middle thirties.

It will be gathered that *Synge and Anglo-Irish Literature* is in many respects scarcely happier in critical scholarship than its bulky predecessor, *The Hidden Ireland*. Even when it comes to right judgments, it seems to do so for the wrong reasons. And as usual in his polemical writing, the author is wordy and repetitious in a schoolmaster's insistently dogmatic way; he can even sink to a surly tone in his remarks on Synge's great-grandfather. In short, it would be hard to disagree with Price that this book is "most provoking," and that the author's "final impression about Synge, that there was considerable power which went largely to waste because of racial and religious bias, is really much more true of Corkery than of Synge." But there is little point in belaboring this critical nag further. Instead, let us glance at the kind of thinking which characterizes the book, which is speckled by recurrent, and extravagant, plugs for Irish as a language.

Corkery gets under way by damning those Irish nationals who write primarily for a non-Irish public and not as nationalists, and who don't come running home to join in revolution or contribute to political funds. For the Irishman, in his view, "feels it in his bones that Ireland has not yet learned how to express its own life through the medium of the English language." (At this point one wonders why Corkery, then, sought American and British markets—and what niche he may have reserved for such an artist, say, as Joseph Conrad.)

After discriminating "the Irish national being" on the grounds indicated by O'Hegarty, Corkery divides all Anglo-Irish literature into "the literature of the Ascendancy writer and that of the writer for the Irish people." Presently he is suggesting that Synge's experience of the Continent brought him to Nationalism and Nationalism "made the difference in what he wrote before and after his visits to the Aran Islands." (Often the book veers into propaganda, as for example in its praise of the Gaelic League.) Corkery seems to read assumptions into Synge and then belabor him as having justified them. He attacks the playwright as one who demanded only imagination in drama; he quibbles argumentatively that both symphony and drama are didactic in that "they open up new horizons, they release new powers within us"! One gathers that Corkery could be as capricious in definition as his purposes demanded.

Presently he is asserting that Synge's view of the importance of imagination led him, except in *Riders to the Sea,* into "cheap things"! A good deal of what follows is really rooted in the to-Corkery-obnoxious fact that Synge was a totally nonpolitical person who came out of a Protestant Ascendancy tradition, though he *had* achieved a degree of saving grace by learning Irish. The consequence is absurdity piled on absurdity, as when

Corkery finds "an air of moral irresponsibility in nearly all of" Synge's work, being obviously unable, or unwilling, to distinguish between the nonmoral and the immoral, the personal voice of the dramatist and that of invented character. Again, he blames Synge for not recognizing the "living faith in another world" and showing this in his characters (whose curraghs, even, were "fashioned . . . by . . . inherited faith"!) , such a person as a faithless or agnostic Irishman being in Corkery's view practically a contradiction in terms. He objects to the "flippant use of holy words" by dramatis personae, and even, in a splurge of willful bathos, claims that the phrases Synge took from the people for his work should be regarded "as an index to the state of lyric excitement into which his conversion to Irish nationalism had thrown him"! He goes so far as to refer Synge's natural imagery to his "nationalism." But he doesn't acknowledge Professor Weygandt's having preceded him in pointing the possible debt of Synge's language to George Borrow's. (Cf. *Irish Plays and Playwrights,* Boston and New York: Houghton Mifflin, 1913, p. 179.)

For the rest, Corkery manages to misinterpret one of Synge's famous dicta about poetry, pays qualified tribute to the essays, gives the plays quibbling analysis (perhaps fighting an inner impulse toward unseemly approbation?) that yields only *Riders* . . . the accolade of "almost perfect" but must concede the whole group "unified in mood . . . solid in texture." He minimizes *Poems and Translations* fairly enough, and does grant that Synge "may be counted as one of that small band of writers who began the movement to restore the note of intensity to English literature." In conclusion, he reiterates "Only for the fact that there was a nationalistic movement in the land when Synge returned to Ireland he would never have come to write *Riders to the Sea*," proceeding thence to one more assertion of the necessity for reestablishing the Irish language in the land. Nevertheless, I for one find it hard not to feel that Corkery forced himself on moralistic religious grounds to fault the work of one whose achievement may have been aesthetically, but obnoxiously, appealing to him.

The year after publishing this volume, Corkery declined an invitation to a founding membership in the Irish Academy of Letters, considering the body "doubtfully 'Irish' " and insufficiently concerned with contemporary writing in Irish. But how could he have accepted after the *Synge?* His associates would have been "Anglo-Irish" writers, and was he not capable of asserting (in a review of Seymour's *Anglo-Irish Literature, 1200–1582*) that (despite his own use of the phrase!) Anglo-Irish literature "has never . . . looked at itself, has not established moulds. It would therefore be hard to prove that it exists at all"? (If it doesn't, of course, Corkery's own creative work doesn't exist and there is no excuse for the present monograph.) However, as an *Irish Times* columnist phrases the common recognition, "Corkery's fame lies in his own writings in English"—in what Stephen Gwynn accurately designates his "native language." Incidentally, his position would seem to have made his large amount of reviewing--in

New Ireland, the *Irish Press,* and other journals, as well as over Radio Telefís Éireann—something of a self-delusion whenever he approved such work in English as that of O'Kelly, Stephens, and L. A. G. Strong. In passing, one wonders about the possible significance of the fact that de Blacam does not include him among the "Writers of the Renaissance" in his *Gaelic Literature Surveyed.*

IV

The years of teaching at University College, Cork, saw no diminution in what even generous inclination can hardly call anything but Corkery's linguistic and political fanaticism. In 1933 he was urging that the Gaelic League should "be given over entirely into the hands of young men" (*v.* "What's Wrong with the Gaelic League") ; by the forties he was, *writing in English,* asserting, "The English language, great as it is, can no more throw up an Irish literature than it can an Indian literature. Neither can Irish nationality have out its say in both English and Irish." (Cf. *What's This about the Gaelic League?*) Meanwhile he produced a mass of miscellaneous journalism ranging in topic from Cork's projected town hall to approval of Jack Yeats's paintings and to frequent book reviews. These last are always, if not acutely subtle or stylistically remarkable, at least forthright and broadly competent except when infused with linguistic prejudices or when dealing with an author—for example, Liam O'Flaherty—whose work seemed to him to be coarse, rough, or brutal. Meanwhile, too, he retired frequently to the contemplative pleasures of his painting, of which the *Sunday Independent* once justly remarked, "as in his short-story writing, atmosphere is the dominant factor." And in 1935 occurred one of those untrumpeted kindnesses for which he is specially remembered. His protégé Seamus Murphy, having completed his sculptural training in Paris, had returned commissionless to Cork; Corkery, to help give him a professional start, therefore commissioned the bust which has earlier been referred to as standing in the Crawford School of Art.

In 1939 came another collection of short stories, *Earth out of Earth,* as well as the production by the Abbey on 28 August of *Fohnam the Sculptor*,* a play which had evolved out of the early *Israel's Incense,* and which in its apparently final manuscript is dated 1938, Ovens. In regard to *Fohnam,* it is perhaps fair to recall what was said of Corkery as dramatist twenty years earlier in the *Irish Statesman*: he has "qualities of greatness. He makes artistic mistakes, and some of us do not always agree with his ethics. But he has a sense of dramatic form, of architecture . . . of character . . . of situation, he has courage and he has pity." Indeed, *Fohnam* is not a perfectly constructed play, lacking structural balance in its lengthy "prelude" and three acts, and a degree of inflation is evident in the dialogue; but the work has color and a fascination peculiarly its own, and it suggests a romanticism—perhaps not unaligned with that of the early Yeats—seldom apparent in Corkery's other work. This tragedy of a sculptor whose capricious perfectionism as a king's city-planner leads

---

* Scheduled (1972) for present publication in *The Journal of Irish Literature.*

him from isolated integrity into cruelty, social fantasy, and an aborted affair with the queen, is not helped by imposing a Christian cultural framework on a society basically pagan. But there is poetry interfused with wildness and gentleness, and there is character.

Earth out of Earth, in page proof by June of 1939, reprinted "Children" from *Ireland Today* (June 1937) and three stories—"Vision," "Death of the Runner," and "Richard Clery's Sunday"—from the *Capuchin Annual, 1938,* as well as "The Inspector" from the earlier *Annual* of 1931. The few reviews available to me were in cordial approval, though the book is obviously no *Munster Twilight* or *Stormy Hills*—a fact perhaps underscored by its unsatisfactory sales record. For on 11 December 1947 the Talbot Press declined to reprint it, saying that five years had been required to dispose of the thousand copies originally issued.

The book has among its dry-mouthed, stone-grey, or almost colorless inclusions only a few pieces suggestive of its author's higher levels, interesting in a general way though most of the material is. There is still diversity of character, but less consequence of situation, with strain to suggest more than naturally logical significance. Such stories as "The Old Men Have a Day Out" peter out weakly and prosaically; others (cf. "The Image Maker") fail more subtly. But there are at least four superlative items—not a bad average for any volume of short stories.

Among these are the almost haunting "Death of the Runner," a tale rooted in a father-son conflict and called up by a wake; "Silence," an exercise in surprise;

and " 'There's Your Sea!' "—of a husband whose peace depends upon a return to his mountains. Most original of all seems "Refuge," in which we discover a very old and sick writer, long forsaken by wife and children into the care of a sister-in-law and her daughter in a tenement house, who finds a symbolic "refuge" in talking the dialogue of characters in an unwritten sequel to his romantic novel of fifty years earlier.

In 1947 Corkery retired on a small pension from University College, Cork, and thereafter his financial condition must have been far from easy, since—to judge from miscellaneous preserved records—his royalties were slender enough: for example, a notation dated 24 November 1937 suggests a total of only £8.15.7 for the year. It is easy to understand why he had on occasion to be reminded of income taxes due. The public, characteristically, was much more willing to praise his books and water colors than to buy them. Slight amelioration came on 30 January 1950 when, after earlier application for relief, he was granted "a temporary increase of £50 per annum" in his "superannuation"!

On 13 July 1948, Corkery was made "Doctoratus in Litteris"/*Honoris causa* by the National University; the same year, an eighty-page issue of *An Siol*—a miscellany of verse, fiction, and learned matter—was compiled in his honor (*An Chuallacht Ghaedhealach*, U.C.C.: cf. the review by Blanaid Salkeld, *Irish Writing*, No. 6, pp. 84–85). In this year he moved from Ballygroman to the Metropole Hotel for about a year, going next to Fanal, Bishopston Avenue, Cork, whence he retired to Myrtleville, Crosshaven, County Cork (his address in 1950), where he remained with his sister until they were persuaded by their niece Maureen to move into her home, overlooking the Lee, at 6 Victoria Terrace, Glenbrook, Passage West, County Cork. It is the niece's memory that in his later years he would—sadly enough—not even speak of his old friend O'Connor, who even in his sharp criticism of the Synge volume calls him "the greatest artist of his generation," though, happily, he maintained his respect for his other famous pupil, Seamus Murphy, who in his view had "integrity."

In 1950 he published in New York *The Wager* . . . , a selective edition of his short stories not issued elsewhere. Fortunately, it stirred unanimously strong approval among the American reviewers, as well as in *Irish Writing* (No. 12). On 9 August of the following year, the Taoiseach, then Mr. de Valera, nominated Corkery for membership in the Seanad Éireann, and he remained a member of that more or less august body until 13 July 1954. On 10 January 1952 he was one of four co-opted for membership in the Arts Council by the Ordinary (*i.e.*, Government-appointed) members; the further record indicates that he attended fifteen of the forty-three meetings following his appointment, and that he was not reappointed after the first Council's term expired on 3 December 1956.

In October of 1954 Corkery (who never painted with a commercial purpose) gave by invitation a one-man exhibition of his paintings at the Victor Waddington Galleries, South Anne Street, Dublin; and his niece recalls how—since they were desired—he called for her suggestions to aid him in inventing titles for the pictures! The forty paintings were priced from £7 to £35; and from the check marks on Corkery's copy of the listing, one supposes that thirteen were sold. On his later, and earlier, participation in group exhibitions of the Munster Fine Arts Association, Cork, practically no useful data seem to be available. A description of him at the time of the Dublin exhibition may be extracted from a "Portrait Gallery" sketch about him in the *Irish Times* for 4 December 1954:

> He is a man of middle height whose well-brushed white hair, parted resolutely in the centre, adds a glow to the smooth, ruddy complexion, and sets off the startlingly blue eyes. [Report assigns to Corkery both "brown" and "blue or greyish" eyes!] The face is that of a meditative man whose instinct is for integrity in thought and urbanity in discussion.

That Corkery's water colors, largely of rural scenes in the Lee valley, have never had deserved appreciation is the opinion of the present unqualified judge, impressed by the delicate sensitivity and atmospheric suggestiveness of this work.

Corkery's last literary work of any scope (he did issue *An Doras Dúnta* in 1953) was *The Fortunes of the Irish Language,* published in 1954 by Fallon, of Dublin, for the Cultural Relations Committee of Ireland and reissued as a Mercier paperback fourteen years later.

This work, originally proposed by Denis Gwynn in 1949 as a 15,000-word pamphlet for which Corkery was to receive fifty guineas, is not precisely what its title might lead one to expect, as will appear; but it was extensively reviewed and approved in the *Sunday Press* for 28 November 1954. (Cf. *Studies,* 44.)

The book is not purely, or perhaps even basically, a history of the Irish language except insofar as that relates to the social and political progression which is its broad general concern. And it must be read as the work of one whose approach was that of a willfully romanticizing racist. Corkery inevitably invites skepticism, as when he unqualifiedly asserts, "It is thought . . . that . . . the Gaels brought the Ogham script . . . ," or calls the Brehon Law (presumably based on digests of the laws St. Patrick and his followers approved) "perhaps more ancient than the myths" and dates the overthrow of the language from the annulment thereof, or assigns "the coming of the Gaels" to a period "many hundreds of years before Christ."

For the rest, Corkery writes in miscellaneous fashion of the congeniality of the Latin and Irish cultures and the role of the clergy in preserving Irish literary tradition, recalling the monastic schools and their attraction of foreign students, as well as the privileged activity of a multitude of poets. He is almost childishly concerned to stress the claimed unambiguity of Irish as compared with English. And when he considers the Bardic Schools, he becomes so polemic that subsequent comment on the progress of the language is largely peripheral: "We cannot . . . but think of the unchanging tongue as the very life and soul not only of the schools but of the whole self-conscious nation . . . in almost every verse of that poetry is the land of Ireland"! He admits that the "mind" of the Bardic Schools "was

inbred, even severely academic," but blames this on
the fact that "they existed in occupied territory—their
nation lacked a state"! But his claim that the "finest
specimens of bardic poetry came out of . . . 1350–1550"
is hardly impressive in the light of Quiggin's researches
("From about the beginning of the second millennium
of our era onwards Ireland loses her high place among
the literary peoples of Western Europe": *Prolegomena*
. . . , p. 90) .

So, then, the wandering theme progresses, with right-
ful blame to Henry VIII and Cromwell and no approval of Daniel O'Connell's encouraging the disuse of
Irish; with assertion of the presumption in legal and
educational quarters from the eighteenth century on-
ward that "the Catholic Irish people did not exist . . .
the Irish language did not exist" until the famine of
1847 really did all but end the language and a "literary
tradition that was so much at one with the religious";
but with approving recognition of the Gaelic League's
eventually coming to the rescue. There is even some
praise for Douglas Hyde, "though a Protestant"!

It is pleasant to recall that his particular Roman
Catholicism did not prevent Corkery from counting
Bach greatest among composers—and even pleasanter
to record that he was honored by a radiogram from a
group of admirers and friends on his eightieth birthday.
Three years later he provided the foreword to Moirin
Chavasse's book on his friend MacSwiney. On 31 December 1964, at his niece's home, he complained of a
pain in his side, lay down on his bed, and died.

Corkery had told his sister (who followed him to the

same grave in St. Joseph's Cemetery, Cork, in 1965)
that he wished only his name and dates given on his
tombstone. Seamus Murphy, who designed and cut the
stone, honored these wishes, adding, as appropriate
decoration, only the incision of an ancient type Celtic
cross.

As is apparent from what has been said, Corkery, like
too many of his fellows, was extremely miscellaneous
in his publications, and only chauvinists will persuade
themselves that uniform excellence marks the entire
corpus. Other readers will be more apt to judge him a
competent playwright, a readable versifier whose appeal
is suggestive of that of Padraic Colum and Seumas
O'Kelly, a biased and verbose scholar, a tedious nov-
elist, a competent but religiously prejudiced reviewer,
a strongly opinionated propagandist, and a writer of
short stories which are in numerous instances so supe-
rior as to argue him one of Ireland's most distinguished
practitioners. His significance lies in the sporadic
quality, by no means the quantity, of his work—work
which has a pervasively rock-grey tone. And perhaps it
is not unkind to reiterate, as in any case one must, that
for all his to-do about Irish as a language ("No native
vernacular, no nation": *The Fortunes of the Irish
Language*), almost all his work, and certainly all that
is likely to count, is in English. In other words, his
achievement clearly contradicts his critical stance.

Repondering the critical, historical, and didactic
work, one inevitably endorses what Benedict Kiely has

said in "Chronicle by Rushlight," one of the very few judicious essays on Corkery: "It is hard to know how to meet the illogicality of a man who writes well in English about Ireland and is then, apparently, prepared to maintain that only writing in Irish can properly express the soul of the Irish people." Fortunately, what is bound to persist in the end is the best of the purely creative work—a little set of plays and at least two volumes of short stories fine enough to stand in the front rank of their category. It was in these that Corkery *really* honored Ireland and his heritage.

Bibliography

1) BOOKS AND PAMPHLETS

A Munster Twilight. Dublin & Cork: Talbot Press, 1916; New York: Stokes, 1917.

The Threshold of Quiet. Dublin & Cork: Talbot Press; London: Unwin, 1917.

The Hounds of Banba. Dublin & Cork: Talbot Press, 1920 (later distributed under dual imprint with Unwin) ; New York: Huebsch, 1922.

The Labour Leader. Dublin: Talbot Press; London: Unwin, 1920.

The Yellow Bittern and Other Plays. Dublin: Talbot Press; London: Unwin, 1920.

I Bhreasail/A Book of Lyrics. Dublin: Talbot Press; London: Mathews & Marrot, 1921.

Rebel Songs (under the pseudonym "Reithin Siúbhalach"). "Printed and Published by The Provinces Publishing Co.," n.d. [1922: Lee Press, So. Terrace, Cork: R. Lankford, printer and owner.]

The Hidden Ireland/A Study of Gaelic Munster in the Eighteenth Century. Dublin: Gill, 1925.

The Stormy Hills. Dublin: Talbot Press; London: Cape, 1929.

Synge and Anglo-Irish Literature. Cork University Press; London: Longmans, Green, 1931.

Earth out of Earth. Dublin & Cork: Talbot Press, 1939.

Resurrection. Dublin & Cork: Talbot Press, n.d. [National Library of Ireland dates its copy "1942?"]

What's This about the Gaelic League? Áth Cliath: Connradh na Gaedhilge, n.d. [N. L. I.: "1942?"]

The Philosophy of the Gaelic League. Dublin, 1948.

The Wager and Other Stories. New York: Devin-Adair, 1950.

An Doras Dúnta ["The Open Door"]. Baile Átha Cliath, 1953. [Cf. review in *Irish Times*, 22 June 1955.]

The Fortunes of the Irish Language. Dublin: Fallon, 1954.

2) SELECTIVE LIST OF REFERENCES

Anon. Obituaries (1 Jan. 1965) : Cork *Examiner, Irish Independent, Irish Press, Irish Times.* [Cf. University College, Cork *Record,* No. 40 (1965), for obituary material in Irish.]

———. "Portrait Gallery." *Irish Times,* 4 Dec. 1954, p. 8.

Boyd, E. *Ireland's Literary Renaissance.* New York: Knopf, edn. 1922.

Breatnach, R. "Daniel Corkery—Creative Writer and Critic." University College, Cork *Record,* No. 40 (1965), pp. 31–37.

Clarke, L. "Daniel Corkery." *Irish Press,* 25 Aug. 1939.

Cleeve, B. *Dictionary of Irish Writers/First Series.* Cork: Mercier Press, 1967; *Second Series, id.,* 1969.

Colum, Padraic. *Crossroads in Ireland* (Part VI) . New York: Macmillan, 1930.

Corkery, Daniel. Reminiscence of Con O'Leary in University College, Cork *Record,* No. 34 (Easter 1959) , pp. 24–26.

Corkery Papers and MSS (to date, 1970, unclassified) . Library, University College, Cork.

Cullen, L. M. "The Hidden Ireland: Re-Assessment of a Concept." *Studia Hibernica,* No. 9 (1969), pp. 7–47.

de Blacam, A. *A First Book of Irish Literature.* Dublin & Cork: Talbot Press, n.d. (? 1934).

de Blacam, H. *Gentle Ireland.* Milwaukee: Bruce Publishing Co., 1935.

Gwynn, S. *Irish Literature and Drama in the English Language.* London: Nelson, 1936.

Hogan, R., and O'Neill, M. J., eds. *Joseph Holloway's Abbey Theatre.* Carbondale and Edwardsville: Southern Illinois University Press, 1967.

Hutchins, P. "Daniel Corkery, Poet of Weather and Place." *Irish Writing,* No. 25 (Dec. 1953), pp. 42–49.

Kiely, B. "Chronicle by Rushlight." *Irish Bookman* 2, No. 4 (Jan. 1948): 23–35.

Kunitz, S. J., and Colby, V., eds. *Twentieth Century Authors/ First Supplement.* New York: Wilson, 1955.

Mac Manus, F. "Three First Meetings." *Capuchin Annual,* 1959, pp. 53 ff.

Malone, A. E. *The Irish Drama.* London: Constable, 1929.

Mercier, V., and Greene, D. H., eds. *1000 Years of Irish Prose/Part I.* New York: Devin-Adair, 1952.

Millett, F. B. *Contemporary British Literature.* New York: Harcourt, Brace, 1935.

Murphy, D. "Donal . . ." *Capuchin Annual,* 1967, pp. 83–97.

O'Connor, F. *An Only Child.* New York: Knopf, 1961. (*N.B.:* O'Connor's *My Father's Son*—London: Macmillan, 1968—has a few passing references.)

————. Essay on Synge in *The Irish Theatre,* ed. L. Robinson. London: Macmillan, 1939.

O'Faoláin, Seán. "Daniel Corkery." *Dublin Magazine* 11, No. 2 N.S. (Apr.–June 1936): 49-61.

————. Chap. 9, *Vive Moi!* Boston & Toronto: Little, Brown, 1965 (Copy. 1963, –64).

Ó Tuama, Seán. "Dónal Ó Corcora agus filíocht na Gaeilge." *Studia Hibernica,* No. 5 (1965), pp. 29–41.

Price, A. *Synge and Anglo-Irish Drama*. London: Methuen, 1961.

Quiggin, E. ("Prolegomena to the Study of the Later Irish Poets 1200–1500," *Procs. of the British Acad.,* 1911–12 (Oxford).

Saul, George Brandon. *Rushlight Heritage*. Philadelphia: Walton Press, 1969. The essay on Corkery has, because of misleading records, one or two biographical errors.